Agnes's Rescue

Whenever I think about pioneers,
I think of brave women and men.
I like to remember
that children came, too;
I would like to have been a child then.
– Della D. Provost
"Whenever I Think about Pioneers,"
© By Intellectual Reserve, Inc.
(used with permission)

The True Story of an Immigrant Girl
retold by Karl Beckstrand & Veara Southworth Fife

For my mother, who brought the stories of her ancestors to life in the hearts of her children & grandchildren - K.W.B.

Agnes's Rescue: The True Story of an Immigrant Girl
Young American Immigrants, Book I (*Ida's Witness* [II],
Anna's Prayer [III], *Samuel Sailing* [IV])

Text & Illustration Copyright © 2021 Karl Beckstrand. Special thanks to Sean Sullivan & Beth A. Lauderdale
Premio Publishing, Midvale, UT, USA
Library of Congress Catalog Number: 2021931888, ebook ISBN: 978-1005577032, ISBN: 978-1975888831

ORDER direct, or via any major distributor.
Libros online books FREE/GRATIS: PremioBooks.com

Other stories by Karl Beckstrand:
Horse & Dog Adventures in Early California: Short Stories & Poems
The Bridge of the Golden Wood: A Parable on How to Earn a Living
Ma MacDonald Flees the Farm: It's not a pretty picture...book
She Doesn't Want the Worms! – ¡Ella no quiere los gusanos!
Crumbs on the Stairs – Migas en las escaleras: A Mystery
No Offense: Communication Guaranteed Not to Offend
Sounds in the House – Sonidos en la casa: A Mystery
It Came from under the High Chair: A Mystery
It Ain't Flat: A Memorizable Book of Countries
The Dancing Flamingos of Lake Chimichanga
GROW: How We Get Food from Our Garden
Bright Star, Night Star: An Astronomy Story
Polar Bear Bowler: A Story Without Words
Arriba Up, Abajo Down at the Boardwalk
Bad Bananas: A Story Cookbook for Kids
Butterfly Blink: A Book Without Words
Great Cape o' Colors - Capa de colores
Why Juan Can't Sleep: A Mystery?
Muffy & Valor: A True Story
To Swallow the Earth

PREMIO
PUBLISHING

My name is Agnes, and this is a story about, well, my feet!
I was born in the beautiful city of Glasgow, Scotland. My mother had come
from Ireland. My Scottish father was lost at sea when I was very young.
It was not easy for Mother to take care of three boys and two girls by herself.
She rented out rooms and fed lodgers. She also made dresses to sell. We
didn't have much growing up—but we were happy!

I can still hear the little girls who would stop at our gate and call, "Aggie t'way, Aggie t'way, are you comin', are you tomin'? Say, 'Aye' or 'nay,' for I'm weary and sleepy and am going away." I would then scamper out and we would chase each other over the vast green by the Clyde River.

I loved to watch the big ships go up and down the river. I would imagine that one was taking me all the way to America.

Before my father died, he and my mother joined the Church of Jesus Christ of Latter-day Saints. My aunts, uncles, and grandmother were Mormons too—and had sailed to America to be with the "Saints." My mother was saving every penny so that we could join the family there.

One day Mother told us, "I've bought boat tickets for us to go to America!" It was then that we learned that my brother William had, on a dare, joined the Scottish army. Mother's heart seemed to break. William had to stay and do his duty—and Mother had a terrible choice to make. If she followed the Saints to America, she must leave her boy behind. Mother's faith was steady; she invited our friend Christena to use William's ticket.

I was nine years old when we set sail with many other Latter-day Saints on the ship Thornton in May 1856. The trip to the United States took almost seven weeks.

We landed in New York, and then rode a train to the end of the line in Iowa City.

KABOOM! It was our first American Fourth of July!

"What are you making, Mother?" I asked. "Wee'rre going ta have an adventure. Robert is making us a handcart, and I'm sewing a tent."

"We get to sleep in a tent!" I told my sister Elizabeth.

"Yes," she said, "but we have to walk 1,200 miles to Utah Territory."

We could only bring what would fit in our handcart. Some people had cows or an ox to pull their carts; but most men and women pulled the carts themselves. Almost everyone else walked.

Not far into the journey the handcarts, made from green wood that had not hardened, began to fall apart. My brother, Robert, was supposed to pull our handcart. But he spent most of the time fixing carts as they broke.

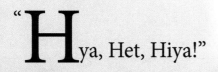

"Hya, Het, Hiya!"

One evening meal was interrupted when some local folks ran off with most of our group's cattle.

M y mother was depending on my brother Thomas to pull our handcart. But, while he was trying to hold a wild cow, his foot got tangled in the rope; he was thrown and broke his collarbone. This meant that Mother and Christena had to take turns pulling the handcart.

BRrrrrmmmmbbbbbbb! A thunder grew to a DIN. We saw the prairie turn dark— "Stampede!" A flood of buffalo tore through the camp, damaging property and sweeping more cows away.

"These delays are dangerous!" said Captain Willie. "Winter will soon catch us."

Walking, walking. My shoes didn't last long. "Dohwn't give up," Mother said. "The Lord will provide." I walked many miles in my bare feet.

It seemed the trip would never end. Many times I became so tired that I would hang onto the cart. But Mother would gently remove my hands. "Darlin' I ca'nuh pull yer weight," she'd say. I would sit down—right there—and cry until everyone was ahead of me. Then I'd have to run to catch up.

We came to a place that was littered with rattlesnakes. My friend Mary and I held hands and made a game of jumping whenever we saw a snake. It seemed we were jumping for more than a mile. But Heavenly Father protected us.

Mother made friends with the Indians. She traded trinkets for dried meat. As our food supply shrank Mother would stew some meat and make a delicious gravy. I guess the reason it tasted so good was that we were only allowed a little bit.

Each day it got colder. By October nineteenth there was no more flour. That night the first snow came—a foot and a half of it. And we still had to cross the Rocky Mountains.

My sister Elizabeth's toes froze. Robert carried her for miles. I wrapped my feet in gunnysacks and kept walking. Soon, we could go no farther.

One terrible night, fourteen people froze. They were buried in one grave.

Elder Franklin Richards, on his way to Salt Lake City by horse carriage, saw our hungry snowbound group. He hurried to The Valley and told President Brigham Young of our trouble. The next day in church conference, President Young asked people to load wagons with food and go to help us.

The rescuers found us by the Sweetwater River. We thanked God for the flour, onions, and clothes that came in the wagons. Many people had not eaten for days.

Elizabeth and others who were frostbitten or sick got to ride in the wagons. Everyone else had to keep walking.

A few of us kids tried to keep up with the wagons, hoping to get a ride—at least, that's what I hoped. One by one, kids dropped out until I was the only one keeping up.

After what felt like the longest chase I had ever made, a driver called to me, "Say, sissy, would you like a ride?" In my best manner I answered, "Yes, I would, sir." The driver reached over and took my hand but, before I could get in, he clucked to his horses—which began to trot—forcing me run on legs that were already spent. It seemed like he held on to my hand for miles. I thought he was the meanest man who ever lived!

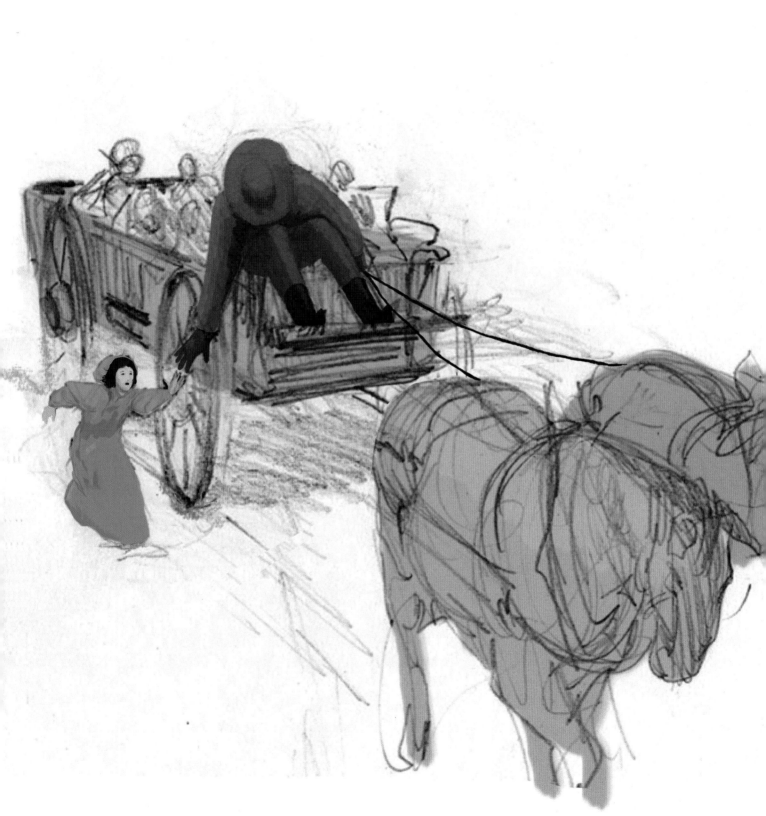

Just when I was ready to give up, the driver stopped the horses. Taking a blanket, he wrapped me up and laid me in the wagon, warm and comfortable. I realized that, by making me run, he had saved me from freezing once I was still.

Along the trail we were met by more wagons. Soon there were enough to carry everyone. We were going to make it to the Valley!

The people of Salt Lake City were so happy to see us; they paraded us down the street. "This must be Zion," I thought. "Everyone is so clean!"

My aunts and uncles found us. They took us to warm homes and fed us.

Because of frostbite, some of Elizabeth's toes had to be removed. But she was soon able to walk without trouble.

It wasn't long before we had a home of our own. The long cold journey was over—but it brought blessings that will last forever. Although I walked much of the way without shoes, my feet didn't freeze. Heavenly Father gave me strength and watched over me—all along the way.

HOW MANY brothers and sisters did Agnes have? (Agnes had an older sister, Mary, who died at 7 months.) WHAT are their names? WHICH two rivers are named in the story? WHAT four cities are named? Name four modes of transportation used to come to Salt Lake City (a handcart is the same as walking). WHERE are your ancestors from? (See FamilySearch.org.) Can you guess the year that Agnes was born? (See the paragraph about the ship Thornton.) HOW many references to feet did you see? Can you think of some blessings that follow Agnes because of her journey? (See some below—plus more answers at PremioBooks.com/online-story-secrets.)

Epilogue

The Willie Handcart Company arrived in the Salt Lake Valley November 9, 1856. LDS Church President Brigham Young told Salt Lake's citizens, "Prayer is good, but when baked potatoes and pudding and milk are needed, prayer will not supply their place…give every duty its proper time and place" (quoted in Deseret News, 10 Dec. 1856).

During the trek, there were three marriages, three births, and close to seventy deaths in the Company. The driver who saved Agnes from freezing was Heber P. Kimball, son of Apostle Heber C. Kimball.

Agnes's grandmother, though eager for her family to join her in Zion, was not there to meet the family. She had taken another voyage—to prepare to greet William and the rest of the family in a Heavenly Home.

Agnes's mother worked to send money to her son, William, so that he could join them after his army service (Crimean War). Very close to his Utah destination, William became ill and died in Wyoming.

In Utah, Agnes Caldwell helped the family by tending sheep and spinning yarn. She loved theater and dancing. She eventually married a fellow actor, Chester Southworth, III, January 1, 1865 in the LDS Salt Lake Endowment House. They had thirteen children (the last of which is author Veara Southworth Fife. Karl Beckstrand is a great-great-grandson through Agnes and Chester's daughter Agnes Southworth Wilcox). Agnes taught school, was a postmistress, and—with her husband—helped establish communities in Utah, Idaho, California, and Alberta, Canada. She died September 11, 1924 and is buried in the Brigham City Cemetery in Utah.

A blessing pronounced on Agnes says, "Thou art one [who] has left thy native land in the days of thy youth and encountered the dangers of a long journey, both by land and by sea, in order that you might find a resting place for thy feet in the valleys of these mountains, where you can be taught to walk in the ways of the Lord." Agnes wrote: "I have often marveled at the faith and courage of my mother in undertaking to forsake her all to be with the Saints."

In the twenty years before the 1869 completion of the transcontinental railroad, more than 70,000 "Mormons" traveled on foot and in wagons from Iowa to the Great Salt Lake Valley (a part of Mexico when the pioneers first arrived in 1847) in one of the greatest overland migrations in American history. The exodus was not entirely voluntary; though devoted to the United States Constitution, the Church of Jesus Christ of Latter-day Saints had not enjoyed its protections. Members urgently needed a home where they could practice their religion free from persecution. Getting to The Valley was only the beginning. The Saints still had to transform a desert. In nearly 400 sites throughout what is today the Western United States, Northern Mexico, and Western Canada, Latter-day Saints planted farms, built roads, waterways, homes, schools, and produced their own clothing. See https://newsroom.churchofjesuschrist.org/article/pioneer-trek

Hosanna, Hosanna!

We've found our new home!

Joy and thankfulness filling their song. - Della D. Provost

Retouched photo of Agnes as a young woman

Made in the USA
Columbia, SC
07 May 2021